Free Verse Editions
Edited by Jon Thompson

ALSO BY SASHA STEENSEN

A Magic Book
The Method
House of Deer
Gatherest
Everything Awake

WELL

Sasha Steensen

Parlor Press
Anderson, South Carolina
www.parlorpress.com

Parlor Press LLC, Anderson, South Carolina 29621

Library of Congress Cataloging-in-Publication Data on File

978-1-64317-439-6 (paperback)
978-1-64317-440-2 (pdf)
978-1-64317-441-9 (ePub)

1 2 3 4 5

Interior design by David Blakesley
Cover design by HR Hegnauer.

Parlor Press LLC is an independent publisher of scholarly and trade titles in print and multimedia formats. This book is available in paperback and ebook formats from Parlor Press on the web at https://parlorpress.com or through online and brick-and-mortar bookstores. For submission information or to find out about Parlor Press publications, write to Parlor Press, 3015 Brackenberry Drive, Anderson, South Carolina 29621, or email editor@ parlorpress.com.

Contents

~~sion~~ of the Feigned hand in which Evelina was written

~~for Disguise to her hand~~

the use of all this? for I'm not enough of a conjurer to find it out."

"Use, indeed, repeated Madame Duval, Lord, if every thing's to be useful!"

"Why, Sir, in regard to that, Sir, said our conductor, the ingenuity of the mechanism —— the beauty of the — the Machine —— undoubtedly, Sir, any person of Taste, may discern the utility of such amazing Workmanship."

"Why then, Sir, your person of Taste, said the Captain, must be either a coxcomb, or a Frenchman: though, for the matter of that there, 'tis the same thing."

Just then, we were shewn a Pine Apple, which presently opened, & discovered a Nest of Birds, who immediately began to sing. "This is prettier than all the rest, cried Madame Duval, I declare in all my Travels, I never see nothing eleganter."

"Hark ye, Friend, said ~~the~~ Captain, hast never another Pine Apple?"

"Sir? —"

"Because, if you have, give it me without the Birds, for, d'ye see? I'm no Frenchman, & should like something more substantial."

This Entertainment concluded with a Concert of Mechanical Music. I cannot explain how it was produced, but the effect was pleasing. Madame Duval was in extacies, & the Captain flung himself into so many ridiculous distortions, by way of mimicing her, that he engaged the attention of all the company; &, in the midst of the performance of the Coronation Anthem, while Madame Duval was affecting to beat Time, & uttering many expressions of delight, he called suddenly for Salts, which a lady, apprehending some distress, politely Handed to him, & which, instantly applying to the Nose of poor Madame Duval, she, involuntarily, snuft up ~~such a quantity~~ that the pain & surprise made her scream aloud. When she recovered, she reproached him with her usual vehemence; but he protested he had taken that measure out of pure friendship, as he concluded, from her raptures, that she was going into Histerics. This by no means appeased her, & they had a violent Quarrel; but the only effect her anger had upon the Captain, was to encrease his diversion. Indeed he

laughs

Contents

...... of the feigned hand in which Evelina was written, to disguise to her Lordship,
the use of all this? for I'm not enough of a Conjurer to find it out."

"Use, indeed, repeated Madame Duval, Lord, if every thing's to be useful!—"

"Why, Sir, in regard to that, Sir, said our conductor, the ingenuity of the Mechanism—the beauty of the—the Machine—undoubtedly, Sir, any person of Taste, may discern the utility of such amazing Workmanship."

"Why then, Sir, your person of Taste, said the Captain, must be either a Coxcomb, or a Frenchman: though, for the matter of that there, 'tis the same thing."

Just then, we were shewn a Pine Apple, which presently opened, & discovered a Nest of Birds, who immediately began to Sing. "This is prettier than all the rest, cried Madame Duval, I declare, in all my Travels, I never see nothing eleganter."

"Hark ye, Friend, said the Captain, hast never another Pine Apple?"

"Sir?—"

"Because, if you have, give it me without the Birds, for, d'ye see? I'm no Frenchman, & should like something more substantial."

This Entertainment concluded with a Concert of Mechanical Music. I cannot explain how it was produced, but the effect was pleasing. Madame Duval was in extacies, & the Captain flung himself into so many ridiculous distortions, by way of mimicing her, that he engaged the attention of all the Company; &, in the midst of the performance of the Coronation Anthem, while Madame Duval was affecting to beat Time, & uttering many expressions of delight, he called suddenly for Salts, which a lady, apprehending some distress, politely handed to him, & which, instantly applying to the Nose of poor Madame Duval, she, involuntarily, snuft up such a quantity, that the pain & surprise made her scream aloud. When she recovered, she approached him with her usual vehemence; but he protested he had taken that measure out of pure friendship, as he concluded, from her raptures, that she was going into Histerics. This by no means appeased her, & they had a violent Quarrel; but the only effect her anger had upon the Captain, was to encrease his Diversion. Indeed he laughs

The background text on the cover is from *Evelina or The History of a Young Lady's Entrance into the World* (1778) by Fanny Burney.

For those who drink from once pure wells
& for my mother, for Becky, for Kristy

my body, a barometer

—Audre Lorde, *The Cancer Journals*

Well

GIVEN: A PREFACE

We all have words we hear as bells, as bellows, as bellwethers.
When these words are spoken, we hear them louder, clearer.
They rouse us from a waking sleep.

You know the words I mean.

Word-bells.

Mostly women have given me my words.
Creek was given. *God* was given. *Garden* was given. *Margin* was given.
My teacher taught me "all words run along the margins of their secrets."
Rachel Carson called the edge of the sea "the marginal world."

 She loved the crabs that scuttled at the margins.

Several years before her breast cancer diagnosis, Carson wrote:
"the little crab alone with the sea became a symbol that stood for life itself—
for the delicate, destructible yet incredibly vital force that somehow
holds its place amid the harsh realities of the inorganic world."
(howls its place)

The little crab is also cancer's symbol.

The margin of a cancerous tumor is removed during surgery.
When no cancer cells are found at the edge of the tissue,
the margin is described as negative.
When cancer cells are found at the edge of the tissue,
the margin is described as positive.

The margin where ill and well meet.

Dying of uterine cancer, Terry Tempest Williams's mother directed her to her journals, though she instructed her daughter to wait until after her death to read them. A few weeks after her mother passed, Williams found the journals, but what she didn't find were words. Her mother's journals, shelf after shelf, were blank.

"My Mother's Journals are the power of absence."
"My Mother's Journals are the power of presence."

After being diagnosed with breast cancer, I began reading the texts of other women writing through diagnosis. I discovered that oftentimes these writers chose to write about their illness in letters and journals, which, presumably, they never planned to publish. Sometimes, even in these private writings, references to the writer's cancer were veiled, secondary, marginalized.

Cancer and *Breast* were given.

I hear these words now and two bells ring as one.

A belling is a welling up of water, as from a spring.

To be made well again, a cancer patient who is also a writer has to gauge
the healing that is done by making her illness her subject versus
the damage that is done by making her illness her subject.
That which cures cancer also causes it.

What is the margin of doubt, the margin of error,
        the margin where to harm is also to heal?

Shortly after I was diagnosed, my friend Julie sent me a copy of
Audre Lorde's *Cancer Journals,* which I read as I recovered from surgery.

"I was going to die, if not sooner, then later, whether or not I had ever
spoken myself," writes Lorde.

But to whom must she speak? The nurse who insisted she wear a prosthesis?
The cancer-industry that demanded she follow its protocol?
The toxic, racist, misogynistic, homophobic world that didn't want her to survive?

To them she rang the word-bell that she meant the rest of us to overhear—*No.*

No was given.

Lorde rang other words as well.

Loneliness was given.
Companionship was given.

As she tells it, never had she been so lonely nor so accompanied, "floating upon a sea within a ring of women like warm bubbles keeping me afloat upon the surface of that sea."

Mostly women have given me my words, and I heard
the books
with all their
beautiful names
ringing
on the shelf.

A few days after Thanksgiving, 1960, Rachel Carson wrote to her friend
(possible lover), Dorothy, to tell her that her breast cancer had spread,
 "I thought a door had been closed last spring, and now it has been opened
a little."

She worried mostly about how this opening might slow her work on *Silent Spring,*
how it might infringe upon her ability to answer "the sense of urgency…
to press on with the things I need to say."

Toxin is given.

In *Silent Spring,* she kept her distance, writing about how chemicals affect
plankton, chickadees, robins, brown trout, whitefish, ladybugs, pirate bugs,
and humans, without ever mentioning the cancer she was battling as she rushed
to finish the book.

Carson felt the mounting pressure to write about carcinogens.
Carson felt the mounting pressure not to write about her own cancer.

What is the margin of exposure, the margin of safety, the margin at which
the toxic becomes carcinogenic, genotoxic?

A woman writing about her experiences runs the risk of being discredited.
A woman writing about her cancer worries she might spread it.

Like the shifting margins we see on the shore—swash lines, bedforms,
drift lines, ripple marks, up and down, up and down the seaboard—
fear strays toward the diagnosed and then away.

"Always the edge of the sea remains an elusive and indefinable boundary,"
                                                    writes Carson.

What if the body is an ocean which, at every tide,
            covers what it needs to survive?
What if the body is an ocean which, at every tide,
            recovers what it needs to survive?

Body is given.
Survive is given.

What if the body is boundless/marginless
            when afloat upon
the boundless/marginless waters?

My daughters watch me as I swim out into the Pacific, past the waves,
            and float, eyes shut.

They dip their toes but do not dare swim in without me watching them.

Women in crisis sometimes address other women (in letters)
or themselves (in dairies, journals, notebooks)
as protection against a world hostile toward their bodies.
Or, they address both.

Friend is given.

They send their message out into the not-always-greatly-hopeful,
            toward something standing open.
They float.

A margin is open, as is a poem.

"Maybe margins shelter the inapprehensible Imaginary of poetry."

Maybe a poem is a margin, a margin a poem.

Growing up, my mother often gave me books as gifts: some empty
(intended as diaries or journals)
some full of words
(*The Tale of Peter Rabbit, Little Women* & *The Poems of Emily Dickinson*),
                                                    all with inscriptions.

Book was given.
Milk was given.
Word was given.

What did *she* call the empty books?
Were they all-open or all-margin?
In them,
I kept
        a list of words
I kept
        quotations
I kept
        quiet
I kept
        writing messages
I kept
        them close to my heart
& sent them off to wash up, perhaps, on some heartland shore.

What do we call the once-empty book now flooded with words?

October 22, 1983:
Today I got my period.

Nothing else is written on the subject, until now:

Finding the green skirt of my Girl Scout uniform turned red with blood,
the troop leader called my mother and said,
"Your daughter became a woman today."

My mother took me home, soaked my clothes in cold water,
and put me in the tub, just as any mother of a young girl would.

      Dear body,

      "Pulse of red on the horizon for the ten minutes after the sun has set.
      …the rim of the mountain behind which the sun has just set
      like the top of a volcano—"

I can no longer find the origin of that quote.

I was nine years old.

Each month, on the horizon, the sun always rising, setting, or erupting.

I have mountains of names to climb (Tetons, Nippletop Mountain, Tetas,
Mammalles, Maiden's Pap, Squaw's Tits) before I find

                        the other side
                        open wide

      thine gaia.

Historically, the letter, the journal, the diary, were genres available to women writers when other genres were denied.

Sometimes, for women, writing letters and keeping written records of daily activities was not only allowed, but required.

Mormon women, Terry Tempest Williams tells us, were expected to keep a journal.

"My Mother's Journals are an act of defiance."

Susan Dickinson, Emily Dickinson's sister-in-law-friend-beloved- co-creator-of-"early-girl-hood-intimacy-"writer-in-her-own-right-constant-correspondent-reader-probable-lover was the first person to refer to Emily's letters as

"letter-poems."

Sometimes women disguise journals as letters,
                    letters as journals,
                    poems as journals,
                    journals as poems,
                    letters as poems,
                    poems as letters.

Sometimes disguised as poems, letters, journals, women open margins
in all directions until the text is all margin, all monstrous. Monstrous
because sender-recipient, self-other, are intimate, are merging. Monstrous
because we don't know what to call *it*.

"My Mother's Journals are letters never written."

Letters are journals never kept.
Journals are letters never sent.
Diaries are days spent in/with
words at the helm out/over
bobbing up and down.

"When I got your letter it looked like a letter I had written to myself
without remembering," writes Bernadette Mayer
in *The Desire of Mothers to Please Others in Letters.*

This way of (not) remembering, of lettering, of reading/writing
to one(another)self(each)other is the shadowside,
the giftside of being a body in/without margins.

My friend Laynie wrote *The Desire of Letters* as an homage to Mayer,
because "you taught me to be presently present."

"So please, partake now and be always well,"
writes Laynie to Bernadette,
writes Bernadette to someone not named.

This, then, is awash
a wash, the well
so many women
held me
in/ from.

Be always well.
Well is given.

I have almost always referred to those once-empty-books-now-flooded-with-words as "notebooks."

Poems are notes that precede and exceed long before they recede to reside in a book that opens to hold them, all margin.

Full of disclosures and failures, disjointed and processual, most of my notebooks are painful to read.

But necessary.

In a 2008 notebook, during a pregnancy I was told may be both cancerous and unviable, I copied the following quote from the "The Uncut Self":

> "full circle, not based on the rectilinear frame of reference of a painting, mirror, house, or book, and neither 'inside' nor 'outside' but according to the single surface of a Mobius strip… Topologically the self has no homuncular inner self but comes… full circle, not based on the rectilinear frame of reference of a painting, mirror, house, or book, and neither 'inside' nor 'outside' but according to. the single surface of a Mobius strip," & so on.

Written collaboratively, the authors, mother and son, chose to begin and end their essay mid-sentence, opening "full circle" as if to draw the whole world to the self, the whole self to the world. Thus, the self is something other than independent and singular. Now I see, when I copied the quote, joining the severed beginning and end without referencing the essay between, I must have wondered if it was time to reconsider what a body might be.

Six months later. Greta. My daughter. Born healthy:
                    of me, from me and altogether, not me.

It took me nearly three years to obtain an image of my cancerous breast.

Though the breast belonged to me, the image, I learned, was not my property.

Nothing looked threatening, instead the tumor resembled an oyster mushroom and the veins, its accompanying hyphae.

My mycelium.

Every three months when new images are created, the mushroom is still gone.

But what is wellness anyway?

To be in the world, and of it?

Or, does wellness mean to be
"in the beached margin of the sea,"
where we are not entirely
ourselves, but microbial, autopoietic,
grassleafy, sea kaley
polygenomic,
a collection of secrets
sent or kept
a letterjournaldiarynotebook
Is a volcano. Is
a kingdom of cinders.
Is a lover.
Is a poem.
Is the recipient internal
or external, or both?
Is a reaching, regardlessand
once one is known, one knows in which ways one is aloneand
once one is alone, one knows in which ways one is knownand

Diagnosis is given.
Gnosis is given.
Given is given.

Aby gave me a poem:

> 'Perhaps we'll open the day's doors.
> And then we shall enter the unknown."

FOR THOSE WHO DRINK FROM ONCE PURE WELLS

I wille make all thynge wele, I shalle make all thynge wele,
I maye make all thinge wele and I can make all thynge wele.

—The Shewings of Julian of Norwich

My body
a barometer

elsewhere, phloem
lift you up

tuber or bulb

the first word
I heard

when I woke
was the nurse's

well, she said
it went

just outside.

At first I thought
a hole

filled with water
a bucket on a rope

my sleeping reach
I guess

but even that
(assumption) seemed

a struggle

what does
the body know

of where it goes
when the breast

is open
eyes closed

there is a fog
unfolding

that sits low
on the foothills

for some days
and nights

for some weeks
and months

the strangest
thing

is the way
words hide.

/

Sometimes it is ok to be afraid
& necessary

I have one hand
with fear

in it

I hold
it out

toward the wilds

the dove
or eagle

the beak
or feet

land
and tear

the branch

to be
in fact

is to be
itinerant

inside
that which is

errant but unable
to move

by virtue
of its holding truth

tight in its fist.

Only one of us
needs

the other,
doctor.

I spend my days
with you

looking out
your windows

my dove hasn't
come back

with its olive branch
but I look out

for her
from my post

on the second floor
of the cancer center

go ahead,
touch me there

here & here & here.

/

A few days before
the diagnosis:

black widow
in the fuse box
hiding from rain
laying eggs

I left you
be.

Now little baby legs
finding their way out
of the perfect egg sac
the shape of an English pea.

Today I bring my boot to your
hourglass
that you might not
bite my cat
my kin
my
self.

I ache too for the rattlesnake
my neighbor smashed

& I ache
from all the ways wounded
meant encircled and hurt
shame rearranged.

The drought has taught me,
soil like skin,
in the living tissues
is speaking a word:

return

pests
what we wouldn't do
to bring you back
(insects, rodents, weeds)

to live

among us
that we might be

made well
again.

/

I speak to everything:
hello there expanse expense
hello there silent spring
hello there dead ringing
hello there black widow
hello there open window
hello there body speaking
hello there new tumor
hello there a word
it will say everyday
from now on
the word being being
hello there
being

hello there
thin layer of soil
over our earth
think layer of soil
layer of skin
think contaminates
think continents
of it

crop spraying
across the street

think no barrier
between

what is soil
skin
but eons
of interactions
lichens too

& bark
& husk
& peel
& hull
& shell
& sheath
& sleeve
& what else covers
and opens itself
at the same time

what else
permeable
what else
person means
to sound through
what else
lodging place
skin and soil alike
what else
bacteria
fungi
algae
what else
blessed springtails
we need
we can't even see
what else
mites born only
in the fallen needle
of the spruce tree
what else
earthworm
what else
earthworn
what else
earth warns us

what else
my birth canal
my chamber
I pray
that my grave
might be ready
to receive me
ill or well
let nothing else
grow here
no not even our own being
no not even our own being
well
what else

/

Writing is first
a search

like a rock in the sea
she
was surrounded by fields
darkening fields

she
loved
all the weeds
all the insects
all the rodents

equally

she
loved what
was supposed
to grow there
flaming cup
of wood lily
100 species of bees

that which grows
collapses the moment
grows not
in competition
but with hands clasped
with permission
with decomposition
fertilizing
not fear
but weed corners
& field borders
&

& the plants
she brought to bear
on our love of dominion
our dominos late
falling our toxic
muscle flexing
our men not
allowed to be
among us
in tenderness:
chokecherry
choke pear
sunchoke
artichoke
chokeweed
choke seed

she placed a seed
 in our backyard
and round it was
and full of nothing
and tall and gray and bare
the sagebrush rose up to it
along the mountain slope
low and purple green
home and food both
for grouse and antelope
deer and sheep
but not food enough
for our meat

the feed took dominion
everywhere
it did not give
of bird or bush
it gave of disease
now the soy

the corn the wheat
spread far and wide
all need us
to intercede

/

I ask,
what would I die for

I would die for
Groundsel
Sweet clover
Field thistle

I would die for
Sodium Chlorate
2 4-D
Dicamba

I would die for
Scarlet Pimpernel
White Prairie Aster
Foxtail

I would die for
Fluzifop
Atrazine
Triclopyr

I would die for
Dandelion
Crabgrass
Willowweed

I would die for
Glufosinate
Siduron
Bensulide

I would die for
Wild Radish
Henbane
Goosegrass

I would die for
Imazapic
Linuron
MCPA

I would die for
Velvetleaf
Lovegrass
Shepherd's purse

I would die for
Benefin
Prodoamine
Dithiophyr

/

The lightbulb flickers.
Is this what
a cell does?

Tumors
just
a hole filled
up.

Tumors, too,
can be tunnels,
portals.

When mitosis
was just
 a metaphor
my body
was like the lightest
fern so many
pinna, pinnule, lobes
trying not to move
so many roots,
uncurling fronds
willing themselves
still.

Now, so many rays
light me up
each morning.

From the inside
I've
one green leaf,
leaflet of a body
a page on which
to write
where I haven't
been
never will be.

I want to speak
on the body's behalf
half permeable
half committed
to its own survival.

I want to speak
to the large eye
opening
projecting its image
a tightly knit spine
across my chest,
each vertebrae a number
the technician speaks

and I am to lie like dead
as they position me
on the machine

Rays, same as the sun made,
Invisible
see into me.

/

I say to myself:
cell, your name

& my mind make
a pomegranate.

How to imagine you
doing your work?

How to think of you
building yourself anew?

How to speak your name
without becoming a snake?

What color your membrane?
What shape?

At the extremity of this life
there is a question.

The things below
are the things above.

The harmed ozone.
The poet who knows

there is no invention
to behold.

DEAR MORNING, TO WRITE IN PRESENT TENSE IS TO INSIST
WE STILL EXIST

11/20/16

This morning when the doctor calls with the results of my biopsy, I learn, unequivocally, that the self is, and is not, the body.

In all my years of life, I have glimpsed this maybe once,
maybe twice, maybe three times.
Maybe while giving birth. Maybe while being born.

Otherwise, as if a stranger to myself.

I go through the possibilities, laying each one flat on the ground before me.

Maybe I will die soon.   Maybe I will live awhile.

Maybe I will be ill, and then well.   Maybe I will "sail" through.

Whatever the case may be, I am now caught up in the cancer industry,

                              which at every turn,
                              sees cancer it must cure.

11/22/16

I'm cancerous, far & wide!

 I've had all my life, and I will have, a breast I trust, though once a cell
slipped by (survived, multiplied) probably when I was busy, occupied,
feeding babies, I guess.

It knew what it was doing, maybe the bird knows too, sometimes & necessary
to hear this: the air needs us (& the sea & the tree)

not just to be us but to be aware:
there are things that harm and cure.

Jesus says somewhere: the bird doesn't fear the expanse of air, the expense
of being permeable. It doesn't worry over its body or it's branch, both noun &
verb, something heard, something hard.

The healer knew immediately which side had been harmed & begged me,
                                                    repeat it:
                                                    Left.

11/23/16

It seems you (tumor) existed for many years, unbeknownst to me.

Now you (tumor) are nothing if not real, a stone just under the skin.

I study you (tumor) by taking two fingers to my left breast, but not forcefully,
as if to do so might give you (tumor) permission to spread.

I try to commit you (tumor) to memory but instead I think only of brushing my
fingers across the grey-white marble tombstones in Rome's Protestant Cemetery

where
long before you

(tumor)
I did not dare

(tumor)
touch Keats's grave

lest it spread
his fate.

11/28/16

Dr. James M. Dickinson,
looking at my husband,
but ostensibly addressing me, says:

> "I would encourage you to consider a double-mastectomy and implants
> of whatever size you choose.
>
> You are still young and pretty and will want to wear a bathing suit."

11/30/16 (MRI)

> *I die every day!*
> 1 Corinthians 15:31

Praise be to God, my body has become an object!

Here I am and I am   solid.

    I shall not be moved

    I am as a TV mounted on a wall.

    I am as a piece of tinfoil, balled.

    I am as my dog in his deepest sleep.

    I am as a dead weight.

    I am as waiting for nothing to change.

    I am as shot through with beams.

    I am as tissue pinpricked with light.

    I am as the night without a star.

    I am as a car filled with daughters.

    I am, as they say, needed,
            and the needed thing can't go away
            without tucking in its pocket
            that other solid thing—the day.

Who can do all the chores with such efficiency, and occasionally, even grace?

Who can open the jar of pickles?

Who can tie the shoe?

Who can follow the sleepwalker up the bunkbed ladder?

Who can calm the raging storms of morning?

Who can be the *as* that means not just "in similarity,"
                    but also "simultaneously?"

This year the peonies barely bloomed.
The hydrangeas too.

An underthirst
of vigor seldom utterly allayed.

Why aren't you ever afraid, my daughter asks me?

            I die every day!

            I sit down in my cellula
            and pray.

12/1/ 16

Were you raised on a farm, my oncologist asks me at today's appointment.

Not a *real* farm, but one in which my parents grew vegetables and traded with the neighbors.

But across the way, the farm dusters sprayed.

Ah-ha, he says.

This both infuriates me: his surety.

And comforts me: it wasn't something I did, but something I witnessed.

Cancer, the constellation, resembles the letter Y.

It holds the Beehive Cluster, home to over 1000 stars barely visible from earth.

Ptolemy called the cluster, "the nebulous mass in the breast of Cancer."

Early Chinese astrologers said the cluster resembled a demon riding in a carriage.

"Bright star," Keats writes, "would I were steadfast as thou art—"

Potentiality and metamorphosis mark the breast, its cells always ready
to transform themselves to make milk.

A cloud of pollen blown from willow catkins.

Aeolus and his winds. Cipher. Zero. Sign.

The disease takes its name not from the constellation, but from the crustacean.

12/8/16

What do the crab and the disease have in common?

The answer to this question, not unlike the "best" treatment,
depends on who you ask.

 Hippocrates was the first to call cancer "karkinos."

Maybe the cancerous tumor reminded him of the hardness of the crab's shell.

Dissecting a tumor some five centuries later, Galen noticed the veins around
the mass extend out like a crab's leg.

Both pinch hard.

Both scuttle across the floors of silent seas, a secret.

12/20/16

Surgery & your 41st Birthday.

While Rachel Carson was in surgery, Dorothy wrote her a letter:

> There is not a moment when I am not sending you waves of thought
> to strengthen you and hasten your recovery. Of the operation itself
> I have decided to shut it out of my mind as much as I can. We can
> talk *together* maybe you will want to tell me what it means to you.

While I am in surgery, Becky, you are celebrating your birthday &
nursing a newborn baby.

Here's where I answer what has been asked of me:
what is the nature of our connection, Becky?

Lorde: "the erotic functions for me in several ways, and the first is in providing
the power which comes from sharing deeply any pursuit with another person."

well of replenishing, nursemaid of knowledge

                                                          erotic

We can talk *together* maybe you will want to tell me what it means to you.

12/22/16

After anesthesia, words are forgotten.
I want to say *coincidence* but instead, *collateral.*
I want to say *dream* but instead, *dreary.*
I want to say *lunch* but instead, *lurch.*

Thankfully, I can read.

Wrapped in ice and lavender, I read this from Lorde's *Cancer Journal*:

> Throughout that period, I kept feeling that I couldn't think straight,
> that there was something wrong with my brain I couldn't remember.
> Part of this was shock, but part of it was anesthesia as well as
> conversations I had probably absorbed in the operating room
> while I was drugged and vulnerable and only able to record
> and not react.

The words I can't exchange.

Kathy Acker: "Cancer became my whole brain."

Unlike so many of my female friends and acquaintances, I never was "raped,"
but there were other "violations."

A tree full of singing grosbeaks, off-season.

12/25/16- 1/1/2017

On Christmas Day, 1960, Dorothy wrote to Rachel, "This morning I relived with my diary the Christmases since I have known you."

Suppose these are

                                          holy days

to be carried through

                                          &,

 we hope,

                                          known.

Suppose, too, all pain & loneliness,

                                          quieted by snow,

all time passing, not mine alone.

1/5/17

Where is the tumor now, my daughter asks.

No matter how biopsied, measured, located, removed, the tumor remains
one of my body's most successful secrets.

My surgeon, who is also a potter, tells me she knows she's removed
it not by looking, but by feeling.

I think of the boy who first touched this breast.

Serapio Andrade.

His name means bright, solar.

The water in Lake Mead lapping at our feet, clayish.

Clannish, this band of "survivors" with their ribbons and affirmations.

A word that denies that we all die.

1/15/17

Today I receive four pinprick tattoos, which the radiation therapists will use to position my body.

I'm lifted up, shifted down, pushed to one side.

Most easily done, they tell me, if I relinquish control.

I am told one patient used his utilitarian tattoos as the basis for a new decorative tattoo.

His radiation dots subsumed into the eyes of a smiley face on his left hip.

This new tattoo issued the ultimate Fuck-You to all who would aim their rays at his cancerous prostate.

1/18/17

When it comes to conventional cancer treatment, everything that cures also harms.

Paradox is the poet's home.

When I lay my naked torso down each morning on the harm-cure machine,
I want nothing more than to write poems.

But I am told not to move.

Not to speak.

I am, however, allowed to breathe, and breathing is its own kind of poem.

1/23/17

Before the harm-cure machine opens its roving eye, the therapists leave the room
 and walk down a winding hall that is more like a tunnel.

From their control room, they monitor me via closed circuit TV and a camera
bearing the name of the digital imaging company that designed it: *Apollo.*

God of sun and light, plague and healing, music and poetry.

Apollo's precursor, Paean, healed the gods, and as a result,
                                  he himself became a song.

1/25/17

Perhaps most Americans hear the word "Apollo" and think: Outer Space.

I hear the words "Outer Space" and think my body
and that which impresses its damage upon me.

In ancient Macedonia, Apollo (pella) meant stone.

Hard, like a tumor.

On that first morning, Kristy in the waiting room, I read the word *Apollo*
 again and again until treatment ends.

Each subsequent morning, I greet him silently.

Hello my Apollo, I breathe.

1/30/17

With the god of watchfulness watching me, I remember Keats's *Hyperion*,
picked up again but never finished, twice.

In the final lines of the second *Hyperion*, Apollo learns that death
is not the opposite of life.

Instead, it is its entry point, leaving so much birthing and dying to be done
while one is still alive.

"Die into life," Keats writes.

Apollo, flush, "with a pang / as hot as death's is chill, with fierce convulse,"
shrieks, and the poem
                                        "Celestial—"

ends, a death and birth itself, or neither, or the moment just after,
or just before.

My friend writes of Keats's *Hyperion,* "beauty is the very record
of cosmogonic crisis."

But it is also its impetus.

The Greeks win the battle not because they are strong,
but because they catch the Persians off-guard by singing a beautiful song.

2/14/17

I perform the pathetic fallacy:

to the west, the foothills mass together like women lying on their backs
at the beach.

Roundish mounds, not mountains with their achy points,
not newly sprung buds,
not flat chests,
not one breast.

But many. The skyline and my body: barometers of what is to come.

The weather sits there, sometimes clouds obscuring the mounds,
sometimes so blue it aches to see.

Often something in between.

On the other side, you will find water but you have to climb.

6/25/17

We love so much about water, and now this: water, a compression sleeve
for the entire body!

The swollen, radiated breast says, *submerge me so I can rest.*

When I am not tilting my head to breathe, I am the expanse below and between
each stroke.

The Bardo.

Green the earth, green the water, green the color of birth, and below, dark.

Name writ in.

I turn and breathe.

Swimming is one way to say to this particular moment: we still exist.

DEAR YEARS BETWEEN,

one afternoon (May 12, 2018) I was weary and I laid down on rough seas to read
Fanny Burney's account of her mastectomy

through the cambric meant to prevent her from seeing, she saw
                                    "Bright…the glitter of polished Steel—

I closed my Eyes."

In my dream o

                                    fnakedBreastandShoulders

tumorsgrowlikeDandelions
Seedsup againandblowign, justwodays
Afterploweddown

breastsmay havebeen symbolsoffertility since
                                    Romantiquity and theymay have representedthe

powerwomen embodiedbut notforFannyBurneyand
notforme

theywere then heavywithmeaning
theywere then almostthe oppositeof thesethings

oarweeds, the shadow they cast
blowing

Dear Becky,

Do you remember the night we drove up
the road from Jender's apartment

to the base of those Montana foothills
and turned the car off and the brights on

and danced in the dirtspotlight?
Was there a song playing

or did we imagine music? It wasn't
until after we had children

that I came to see, and after
I had cancer that I came to feel,

that the body doesn't so much move
as it is moved through.

I don't know that I have ever
had such trouble

finding a form that is
as amorphous as what I now mean.

Rachel Carson wrote, "the balance of nature is not
status quo; it is fluid, ever shifting,

in a constant state of adjustment,"
by which she means be careful

what you wish to eradicate
because the environment

has its own plans and guess what?
No one knows the extent

to which a species might
reproduce in an environment

without predators
until that environment exists and then,

a sea full of immortal jellyfish
through which to swim.

Something similar can be said
of the cancer cell which does not know

when to die,
when to stop dividing.

When we were washing boats
on Lake Mead, in the desert sun,

we were using our bodies
to earn money

to move the ocean, the pine trees,
the mountains, the geysers, the sulfur springs

through our bodies,
to relieve them of that heat.

When we had enough money,
finally,

we drove up the coast, slept in tents
and in friends' apartments.

We woke one morning
to find cows mulling

about in the foggy sea air,
and we believed we were moving

through that same air too,
it was cool and heavy.

And then we returned
the desert to our bodies,

we returned
during a downpour that flooded

the same streets we left behind
a month before, dry as a bone,

which isn't dry, of course,
unless it is outside the body, bleached

by the oppressive heat that seemed
to accompany us as we worked.

In truth, the heat didn't so much keep
us company, as it was us,

though there was no way
for us to know it back then,

swimming in Lake Mead,
shuffling in and out of air-conditioning.

Now it seems the body
has a way of holding us to it

whether by obligation or approximation,
almost equal to the air it breathes.

After so many years of imagining
my body as something held together

by all the will
I could muster,

I see now that we can't
do anything, exactly,

with, or to,
or for, our bodies.

I see now that
no matter how many times

you move the squirrel around the log,
there isn't a preposition that comes close

to describing what it means
to be embodied.

In graduate school, I was impatient
with the insistent interest in the body.

The body without organs.
The gaze that turns the body into an object.

I wanted nothing more than to use it
to get from one place to the next.

If we had exchanged letters, Becky,
they may have been caught

enclosed in envelopes,
kept in tidy boxes,

but instead I wrote poems
for you, and I read them aloud,

which doesn't surprise me because
we have a history

of being bodies together,
next to one another.

Your room next to mine,
a shared wall.

Now it seems we are sitting
on the edge of overgrown,

this one world's entry point
not the garden

from which we've been thrown
but the body entire,

the entire body, all open
and therefore weary.

World without border,
world before us that is us,

there can be no choice,
there never was a choice,

but to permit thee entry,
and there can be no testament

there never was a testament
to this, but this.

Our wherewithal,
us herewithall

where we've been all
allentire, allalong

together,
togather

/

In a "Journal Letter"
to her sister, Esther,

Fanny Burney wrote:

to meet the coming blow;—

 she would "assume the best spirits" for herself and her
"too sympathising Partner,"
who was sent away on surgery day,
he being unable to steel himself
away, and yet she
          "and self-given up," stayed.

What body-self isn't fictive?

the one who holds
her own breast
as it is cut off
the one who, in the journaletter to her sister, writes:
          "I dare not revise, nor read, the recollection is still so painful."

Keep

Fanny Burney was given her father's permission
to keep a journal if she kept it hidden.

what is the difference between a woman's letters and her journal?
what is the distance between a woman's letters and her journal?

what is the distance between
two women writing letters?

that so many cancer patients write about *the shadow*
cavernous with caverns in me

                                      theselfcave.

what do a journal, journey, diurnal, jour, hour have in common
but the common world?

what collection of tissue in formation (geese), what opening opens
to each leaf each day
what provides more shade until the end of spring?

or was that a dream?
the hummingbird does not so much hum as screech

that's its normal being

blacktailed or broadchinned each gleaning, canopying
what else grows in the body unknown or divides or dies?

what color this hour seems, seams bleeding, much of the body, pink
the way dreams and reading merge?

I write to you to expel the barrier between.

Dear year(s) between,

It is spring and it is blooming
all these birds and their racket

and yet the body-self *is* still
permeable, continuous

with the world
all the nuthatches gone

might sing me a song
of healing.

A hymn
exists

not just
to praise gods

but to heal them
by which I mean Paean

Physician of the gods
Holy-magic-song-singer-seer-doctor

Sings.

/

"This unholy granite substance in my breast," writes Alice James
in a New Year's Day journal entry, 1892, is also holy:

> As the ugliest things go to the making of the fairest....the story of
> [Katherine's] watchfulness, patience and untiring resource cannot
> be told by my feeble pen, but all the pain and discomfort seem
> a slender price to pay for all the happiness and peace with which
> she fills my days.

Katherine was Alice's lover and dearest friend.

                Love.

Untiring Resource.

                Growing, like a tumor.

/

Becky, I keep nothing closetome but mybreast, "mybestfriend," a phrase girls
have been saying for decades &

decades.

This is a love poem,
but not that kind.

Perhaps
in some
other life

you've seen me
break down

& cry.

The Walk

for Kristy
& for Hana, Phoebe, Greta and Iris

When the page answered, so did the larks and the long-
awaited mountain we climbed, many times, but
had not fully seen, its streams, for example, or the river
they feed, or the animal tracks we photographed
but forgot to look up, or track down, or when we saw
what seemed to be a bobcat, or was it a lynx
or a mountain lion, we chose the median,
one having appeared in your dream, its tail we saw
differently—me: black-tipped; you: white underneath,
and having loved the word *lynx*, the word almost without
vowel, the word asking why, when so few words do, so few
willing to betray themselves in this particular way.

Why it was hard to see, exactly, I cannot say, but there was
a way in which we had become preoccupied by our daughters,
it was as if the page, and the word, could not bear it any longer,
this necessary releasing into the world. It was as if
the cliff we often climbed was not able to face
the water below, its mirroring, its sparkling, its overcasting
shadow, as if the coyote we once saw running knew to move
away from us as we opened our hearts to triumph
when triumph meant twilight, or was it dawn when we turned
to our next life with a willingness to be unwilling to be in agony
any longer, the ache the foot felt whenever it touched the runway,
its black asphalt left to crack after too many planes, wind
at their wheels, refused to land on that treacherous path,
so we moved, remember, toward grief, and then I guess
an opening, like the one we once found in the meadow,
or was it a field, a clearing, no doubt, each
flower working its white petals out of the ground, were they
starflowers, or were they some sort of yarrow,
either way, they answered, not unlike the columbine
we passed at the treeline, its open, purple mouth also asking why.

We thought, at first, it was a way to pass the solitude
together, a sort of rhythm to the day that gave

way to the heavy restlessness we both felt,
not unlike the mountain clouds forming
over the house and turning, suddenly, to snow
or rain, everything dreary and glistening, skimming even
the surface of the pond the lightning lit up when we believed
the thunder was further, like the thunderous pain
we shared when we could not possibly share it with them,
our daughters, stuck in the house, and then, walking out.
We always took the dogs, the only ones who seemed
genuinely happy to walk alongside us, their muddy paws,
goatheady, heavy with running, with prairie-dog-longing
with digging for voles or tugging feathers from the already
half-eaten magpie-wing in the sandy-wet soil
at the edge of the barbed-wire fence. That reminds me:

remember when we felt the bird overhead but looked instead
in the opposite direction and were unsure if the sweep
was an owl's or a hawk's, the sun blaring, obscuring
belief like the lynx in the foothill's shadow
where the reservoir's runoff collects,
by the Natural Resource Building. It isn't as if
we always walked in some remote place, in fact
we mostly did not, why I'm not sure, but likely
we had to return quickly to our daughters,
the collected house-finch's nest built on the eaves
nestled between the inherited, useless satellite dish,
its unworldly-blue eggs and the cowbird's single speckled one,
the nest almost blown off for a whole howling spring month
while her younger self marveled and checked every day
for hatchlings that never came, until we brought the nest in
and positioned it on our most visible shelf where it still
sits, its mud, its twigs with dry buds, falling off,
the way after years of why, this just appeared
on the page, water from the rock, my friend,
the walks, the dusk, the dawn, the grey light,
depending on the season, the freeze or heat,
appearing or disappearing, water from the rock,
my friend, the ever-bearing walk we still, to this very day,
take.

Dear year(s) between,

It is autumn
again

I am among the dying leaves,
distrusting

the person who utters the word
death.

What dies not before my eyes
but before my breath?

I am now unable
to do the most basic

tasks, like shitting or
thinking without also

being dead myself
to the very day

the birdfeeder goes
empty by the grace

of one darkeyed
junco at its foot.

Along the way
to fill it

myself
in this altered state

I, obedient to the body of some
more important creature—

one bluebell unafraid
one oasis of beryl

one grouse cock of the plains
—open wide,

 the only way to be alive

Dear Becky,

Did you see the white, white moonlight last evening?
The lighted field, the dead grass tips shining?
Quail broods hiding and salmon spawn, too,
in some river starving?
Their little bodies by midnight,
carried along the gravel bottom
or floating as dead fish do
on fire with that same light?

The mayflies. The blackflies. The stoneflies.
The midges, must go.
Just let the underside of leaves grow
where these insects would have clung until dawn.
The white so bright it might slip through
 the leaf's tight pores. It might open the little stoma,
for the leaf to breathe the night air. Or, choke on it.
What do we hear?
The space where the insects once buzzed.

Does anyone love a fly anyway, she asks,
no doubt remembering me swatting at them in the kitchen.
What if we never again see
those little legs rubbing
cleaning their
"diseased" bodies ?
What wealth of them?
What obliteration,
not unlike my own,
comes to claim them?

And the boll weevil,
devouring the cotton,
must go also!
And with them,
inevitably, the fish of Flint Creek:

white crappies, bass and sunfish.
Carp, buffalo and drum fish,
gizzard shad and catfish,
each first turning wine-dark
and swimming about
as if in a daze.

And the fire ants, too, must go!
In our bare feet about to dip our toes
in that cold silvery moonlit water,
the mound hidden well below
the rotted log; they latch on.

If I weep wondering what
will be left to devour my body,
what will the dirt be teeming with
if all the insects are dead,
if all the earthworms poisoned,
I keep encouraged instead.
In each case, they come back,
Legion.
The Ancient Fly.
The Native Boll Weevil.
The Red Ant Eternal does not die.
100,000 float in a mound
on the surface of flood water
living to care for the large blue
caterpillar, who, through mimicry
secures protection for itself
in the red ants' mound
until its wings
open out.

Or, the gypsy moth.
Mother of all moths.
Mouth open wide
to choose not to die,

not to be
sprayed
to oblivion.
Open wide, I said
be born into this
toxic world
and keep
breathing.
At least, please,
keep your mouth
open to receive
the air we once
shared.

Dear year(s) between,

Within myself
a window

opened.

I will not say how I knew
I'd lose you
to

what?

The world?

There are organisms
that lack
a limiting membrane,
like algae
housing herds
of urchins.

Rachel Carson
studied them.

"So intimate
the union,"

she wrote,

"here
the periwinkles
wear
little patches
of pink on
their
shell."

& like mothers.

The body is
the primary image.

Imagine it otherwise
and find

"their growth giving
the illusion

of thousands
of blossoms,

each as large as the tip
of my little finger."

In the notebook,
my handwriting

is such
that *window*

may be *widow*
but I know

a writer is complicit
with her hand.

I am a pupil
of

one-thing-
after-another

her hand less
useful

when there is a
tremor

tumor.

Dear year(s) between,

Bergson said the body

is the primary
image

but what is the basic ground?

The soul in the cells
The soil
The everywhereness of life

rife.

We live in what Rachel Carson calls
a "sea of carcinogens."

Some kinds of fish live
on others

others on others.

I send you out, then,
to the word
world

kin of mine
be well

be bucket
be pulley
be rope.

/

What do the forms of the letter, the journal, the notebook,
                                        the poem blur?
What allows you to be a you
me to be a me:
a diary.

The letter is a volcano.
The journal is
The diary is
The notebook is
The lover is
a volcano.

I've always wanted to write an essay
about my life as a reader
but now the problem of the ego
where self = reader (or mother, or poet, or teacher, or whatever)

or friend.
Imagine:
non-identity,
an organism that lacks a limiting membrane
(Blue-green algae
housing herds of urchins.)

Imagine: to be
separated = sacred

Kingdom of cinders
dissolved
in this particular sea.

/

Whistle, little wit's son,
I am a pupil

of its passing.

How hollow have I found this
piles of years
of notebooks

as in holes,
and how full.

Even you, Becky, living in the city then,
said sadness hadn't so much entered but interred.

Like your Christian's bundle (born
just before my Phoebe):
larkspur, cobbles
all stacked up
& for what?

They are time themselves.
Its like
one
thing
after
an
other
after
an
o

/

In those years, Susan was always railing against the critics.
I hear her voice so often
& Claudia's.

In my essay on shame, I wrote about the shame
of being a woman in a way that suggested
I did not have a right to this shame.
Julie wrote, "You do."

Who is it I have been hiding from?

O'Hara: Just write the poem to *that* person.

Dear Becky,

Despite my being exhausted by long-standing sorrow, and kept by care

> (cure
> from the Latin *cura*
> not fixed forever
> but cared for   attended to   looked at)

I cannot grieve fully.

I realize now that I haven't looked into my daughter's eyes for awhile,
the way a mother does from time to time to celebrate her child's healthy life,
to beg it stay put,

> (here, the double sense of cura
> concern, absorption
> in the world, but also care
> in the sense of devotion—)

not because I was not concerned, absorbed, but quite the opposite
because seeing *yourself* seen *your* guilt *your* complicity
is sorrow from the Old Dutch *sorga:*
 (care concern attention effort

> anxiety fear danger risk difficulty
> mourning worry and only associated
> with *sorry* when the a rounded
> neatly to the long open o.)

And that any mother wouldn't want that great luxury which wonders
at what age this news (threats: men, guns, environment) needs relayed
to her young daughters, by this I mean the luxury to wait.

> (Cure, too, to preserve,
> to cover, to conceal, to protect
> to choose).

There are other threats I have pointed out: allergen, road, lake, pit or hollow
                    (but don't say *grave*)
where your care is itself a hole large enough to swallow
 the girl's dead bird, sparrow, hen, precious plaything of my sweetheart.

I'm really writing to ask you this question:
should I come out in the open flood
and lay my body over
stretch my legs over
let them pass over   my torso
safely to the other side
                    (not become now
                    and care become cure
                    to cover
                    over now   over)

or should I say goodnight, goodbye

STRIPPINGS: AN APOLOGIA

To read the journals Susan Sontag kept during her breast cancer diagnosis is
to read between the lines. For the most part, she goes about her journaling
business—keeping track of observations and conversations, making notes
for pieces she is writing or hopes to write, compiling lists of books she has
read or hopes to read, listing films she has watched or hopes to watch. No
declaration of diagnosis. No accounts of appointments, procedures, pains,
healings. Above a 1976 entry, her son/ editor made note of these absences:
"*[SS made remarkably few notes about her surgery and treatment for metastatic breast*
cancer between 1974 and 1977.]"

Lonely, I read this not as omission, but permission.
I befriend those I read,
we
share initials, nationalities,
we
inhabit a world made of others' words,
we
set up death so that
we

                                        "Death is the opposite
                                        of everything…"
might write it into its opposite,
we

                                        "explode one's subject—
                                        transform it into something else"
want life to be more than being,
we

                                        "want to write something great"
want to do more than speak,
we

                                                    " want to sing"

The closest Sontag comes to writing about her diagnosis is to write about death transformed by gender: "thinking about my own death the other day, as I often do, I made a discovery. I realized that my way of thinking has up to now been both too abstract and too concrete.

Too abstract: death
Too concrete: me

For there was a middle term, both abstract and concrete:
                              women. I am a woman.
And thereby, a whole new universe of death rose before my eyes."

What does she mean, both abstract and concrete?

Is this the condition of living in a body
continually subjected to the violence of synecdoche?

I propose belonging: this sea of entities within & around me.

In what ways is / are
the words put down
sent out
to those
who have known
what it means
to carry many
my cells, mycelium
In what ways is/ are
our bodies
transposed
over those
who have
also known
this middle term
girl
I'm reaching
always towards them
like letters
deep inside
and I'm receiving
the body's teeming
mouth & ground
foot & feather
breast & biome

Language explodes in the face of diagnosis.

Sontag struggled with the relationship between the notebook and the essay. She did not know how to admit the fragment she felt so pertinent to the experience of illness.

 "Decline of the letter, the rise of the notebook! One doesn't write to others any more; one writes to oneself."

Her notebooks say what the essays assay.

"The Aphorism. The Fragment—all these are 'notebook-thinking.'"

While working on an essay on the German writer Elias Canetti, Sontag kept a notebook of "strippings," or notes not used in essays or stories.

Later: "Yes, an essay on aphoristic thinking! Another ending, wrapping up. 'Notes on Notes.'"

An essay she never wrote, or her Journals / Notebooks.

Susan Sontag wrote *Illness as Metaphor* without once mentioning her breast cancer.
Rachel Carson wrote *Silent Spring* without once mentioning her breast cancer.
Audre Lorde wrote about her breast cancer directly and continually.

If "metaphoric understanding…belies medical realities," what plain speaking,
what apologia, what literal language might speak metaphor away?

Rachel Carson: a letter to a lover-friend.
Susan Sontag: a letter to oneself.
Audre Lorde: a letter to the world, whatever the form.

Dear world,
that wrote to me on a sea,
        I have nothing but hope for thee.

Open a door, let the dawn in.
Open a notebook and sketch it.

BY WAITING & BY CALM

O biota,
living surface
of the earth,
& poisons
& sons
we make to quiet
the teeming ground.
House sparrow
immune
& woodcocks,
your clutch
of unhatched
eggs,
lay down with
all the names
for the towering maple.

O bacteria
from which
we all grow,
to which
we all owe
our living
& our dying,
which are
the same
substance.

O microbes
& chromium
& poems,
O early
winter
& late spring.

O dream
& its afterglow.

O part
& whole
the egg
dropping,
the flutter
in the pelvis
& waste
the same
as use
to sound
through
a body
the only
journey
you
& I
can't help
but make
everyday
& finally.

O meteor shower,
not yours to see,
and yet
wake up early
when it can be
yours alone
& the
earth's entire.

O our tampering
with the atom
& our woodlands
without song.

But this one bird,
this one spore,
this one algae
covered in
button-like
scales,
shells its
own self
with all we make
to lay heavy
upon *our*
teeming ground.

O crabgrass
& boll weevil larvae
picked clean
& cotton safe
for harvesting,
carry on,
but leave me with just one song,
pressed between our palms.

Notes and Acknowledgments

More than any other book I have written, this one demands many acknowledgments. Every word was gifted to me by a woman, whether through speech or through writing. The following women deserve particular thanks for their words, and for their care: Fanny Burney, Alice James, Audre Lorde, Susan Sontag, Rachel Carson, Terry Tempest Williams, Bernadette Mayer, Kathy Acker, Susan Howe, Claudia Keelan, Aby Kaupang, Laynie Browne, Haley Hasler, Nina McConigley, Ramona Ausubel, Camille Dungy, Stephanie G'Schwind, Vauhini Vara, Louann Reid, Shelby Montross, Gianna Vivo, Sierra Slentz, Jennifer Johnson, Arin Fordstat, Julie Carr, Elizabeth Sink, EJ Levy, Yvonne Ramos, Nancy Hadfield, Catherine Hadfield, and Mathilde Cohen. Thank you to my daughters, Phoebe Steensen Hadfield and Greta Steensen Hadfield, for teaching me each day what it means to be in relation, generously. And, most of all: Gretchen Steensen, Becky Abraham, Kristy Beachy-Quick. As Audre Lorde says, "without community, there is no liberation."

Thank you to Marius Lehene and Martin Corless-Smith, who both gifted me their paintings, when I was well and when I was ill. Thank you to my friends and colleagues, Matthew Cooperman, Andrew Altschul, and Harrison Candelaria Fletcher. And thank you, Dan Beachy-Quick, my most trusted reader; your words and your friendship buoy me. Thank you, Erik Steensen and Rob Steensen. Thank you, beloved students, for always teaching me far more than I teach you. Thank you, Gordon Hadfield, my love.

In most cases, where there are quotation marks, the writer/speaker is named, though there are a few notable exceptions. "My teacher," quoted in "GIVEN: A PREFACE," is Susan Howe. Lines from Terry Tempest Willaims's *When Women Were Birds*, are found throughout "GIVEN: A PREFACE," and the quote beginning "Pulse of red..." is Susan Sontag's. "The Uncut Self" was written collaboratively by mother and son, Lynn Margulis and Dorion Sagan. All quotations from "STRIPPINGS" are lifted from Susan Sontag's journals, unless otherwise noted. The poem Aby sent, excerpted in "FOR THOSE WHO DRINK FROM ONCE PURE WELLS," was Octavio Paz's "January First," translated by Elizabeth Bishop. Dan Beachy-Quick's stunning book on Keats, *A Brighter Word than Bright*, is quoted in "DEAR MORNING, TO WRITE IN PRESENT TENSE IS TO INSIST WE STILL EXIST."

Thank you to *Tupelo Quarterly, Poetry Daily, Seneca Review,* and *The Ilanot Review* for first publishing work from this collection.

About the Author

Sasha Steensen is the author of six books of poetry: *A Magic Book*, *The Method*, and *House of Deer* (all from Fence Books), *Gatherest* (Ahsahta Press), and most recently, *Everything Awake* (Shearsman Press), and *Well* (Parlor Press). She has published several essays, including "Openings: Into Our Vertical Cosmos" at Essay Press (http://www.es-saypress.org/ep-40/) and "The (Un)familiar Essay" (https://www.tupeloquarterly.com/the-unfamiliar-essay-by-sasha-steensen/). She is a poetry editor for *Colorado Review* and an editor for the Test Site Poetry Series. Steensen teaches Creative Writing and Litera-ture at Colorado State University where she was named 2023 Stern Distinguished Pro-fessor. With her partner and two daughters, she lives in Fort Collins, Colorado. Learn more about her work at https://sashasteensen.com/

Photograph of the author by Gordon Hadfield. Used by permission.

Free Verse Editions

Edited by Jon Thompson

13 ways of happily by Emily Carr
& in Open, Marvel by Felicia Zamora
& there's you still thrill hour of the world to love by Aby Kaupang
Alias by Eric Pankey
the atmosphere is not a perfume it is odorless by Matthew Cooperman
At Your Feet (A Teus Pés) by Ana Cristina César, edited by Katrina Dodson, trans. by Brenda Hillman and Helen Hillman
Bari's Love Song by Kang Eun-Gyo, translated by Chung Eun-Gwi
Between the Twilight and the Sky by Jennie Neighbors
Blood Orbits by Ger Killeen
The Bodies by Christopher Sindt
The Book of Isaac by Aidan Semmens
The Calling by Bruce Bond
Canticle of the Night Path by Jennifer Atkinson
Child in the Road by Cindy Savett
Civil Twilight by Giles Goodland
Condominium of the Flesh by Valerio Magrelli, trans. by Clarissa Botsford
Contrapuntal by Christopher Kondrich
Country Album by James Capozzi
Cry Baby Mystic by Daniel Tiffany
The Curiosities by Brittany Perham
Current by Lisa Fishman
Day In, Day Out by Simon Smith
Dear Reader by Bruce Bond
Dismantling the Angel by Eric Pankey
Divination Machine by F. Daniel Rzicznek
Elsewhere, That Small by Monica Berlin
Empire by Tracy Zeman
Erros by Morgan Lucas Schuldt
Extinction of the Holy City by Bronisław Maj, trans. by Daniel Bourne
Fifteen Seconds without Sorrow by Shim Bo-Seon, trans. by Chung Eun-Gwi and Brother Anthony of Taizé
The Forever Notes by Ethel Rackin
The Flying House by Dawn-Michelle Baude
General Release from the Beginning of the World by Donna Spruijt-Metz

95

Ghost Letters by Baba Badji

Go On by Ethel Rackin

Here City by Rick Snyder

An Image Not a Book by Kylan Rice

Instances: Selected Poems by Jeongrye Choi, trans. by Brenda Hillman, Wayne de Fremery, & Jeongrye Choi

Invitatory by Molly Spencer

Last Morning by Simon Smith

The Magnetic Brackets by Jesús Losada, trans. by M. Smith & L. Ingelmo

Man Praying by Donald Platt

A Map of Faring by Peter Riley

The Miraculous Courageous by Josh Booton

Mirrorforms by Peter Kline

A Myth of Ariadne by Martha Ronk

No Shape Bends the River So Long by Monica Berlin & Beth Marzoni

North | Rock | Edge by Susan Tichy

Not into the Blossoms and Not into the Air by Elizabeth Jacobson

Overyellow, by Nicolas Pesquès, translated by Cole Swensen

Parallel Resting Places by Laura Wetherington

pH of Au by Vanessa Couto Johnson

Physis by Nicolas Pesquès, translated by Cole Swensen

Pilgrimage Suites by Derek Gromadzki

Pilgrimly by Siobhán Scarry

Poems from above the Hill & Selected Work by Ashur Etwebi, trans. by Brenda Hillman & Diallah Haidar

The Prison Poems by Miguel Hernández, trans. by Michael Smith

Puppet Wardrobe by Daniel Tiffany

Quarry by Carolyn Guinzio

remanence by Boyer Rickel

Republic of Song by Kelvin Corcoran

Rumor by Elizabeth Robinson

Settlers by F. Daniel Rzicznek

A Short History of Anger by Joy Manesiotis

Signs Following by Ger Killeen

Small Sillion by Joshua McKinney

Split the Crow by Sarah Sousa

Spine by Carolyn Guinzio

Spool by Matthew Cooperman

Strange Antlers by Richard Jarrette

A Suit of Paper Feathers by Nate Duke
Summoned by Guillevic, trans. by Monique Chefdor & Stella Harvey
Sunshine Wound by L. S. Klatt
System and Population by Christopher Sindt
These Beautiful Limits by Thomas Lisk
They Who Saw the Deep by Geraldine Monk
The Thinking Eye by Jennifer Atkinson
This History That Just Happened by Hannah Craig
An Unchanging Blue: Selected Poems 1962–1975 by Rolf Dieter Brinkmann,
    trans. by Mark Terrill
Under the Quick by Molly Bendall
Verge by Morgan Lucas Schuldt
The Visible Woman by Allison Funk
The Wash by Adam Clay
Well by Sasha Steensen
We'll See by Georges Godeau, trans. by Kathleen McGookey
What Stillness Illuminated by Yermiyahu Ahron Taub
Winter Journey [Viaggio d'inverno] by Attilio Bertolucci, trans. by
    Nicholas Benson
Wonder Rooms by Allison Funk

Printed in the USA
CPSIA information can be obtained
at www.ICGtesting.com
LVHW070626240924
791861LV00005B/6